MW01059476

FAMILIUS

Published by Familius LLC, www.familius.com
Familius books are available at special discounts for
bulk purchases for sales promotions or for family or
corporate use. Special editions, including personalized
covers, excerpts of existing books, or books with corporate logos, can be created in large quantities for special
needs. For more information, contact Premium Sales at
559-876-2170 or email specialmarkets@familius.com.

Library of Congress Cataloging-in-Publication Data
2015955952
Print ISBN 9781942934417

Printed in China

Edited by Brooke Jorden
Cover design by David Miles
Book design by Brooke Jorden and David Miles

10 9 8 7 6 5 4 3 2 1

First Edition

# OLD AGE

## IS THE ABSENCE OF YOUTH

## (AND A LOT OF OTHER THINGS)

## 175

### *Jokes*

for people who think
napping is a hobby

GENE & LINDA PERRET

Age has become the great scapegoat of our time. If a man goes to a doctor and complains that his right shoulder aches, the doctor may probe around a bit and then proclaim, "It's old age." The man objects, saying, "My left shoulder is the same age as my right shoulder, and that one doesn't hurt at all."

Grouchiness is blamed on aging. Forgetfulness comes with aging. Aches and pains are all considered a result of growing older. It's the wrong approach.

Age is not a villain; it's a blessing. Think of all the lovely songs you've heard the birds sing on crisp mornings. Remember all the friends you've shared happy times with. Even those chums you can't recall are worth remembering. Think of all the flowers you've watched blossom over countless springs. Think of all the wondrous sunsets you've enjoyed. Consider how fortunate you've been to be visited by your children, and their children, and maybe even their children's children. Recall the happiness in your heart when they arrived . . . and, of course, when they went home again.

Growing old gracefully is a privilege. So what if you've been doing it longer than a few other people? Be proud of it.

Remember, too, that we're supposed to grow wiser as we grow older. Even if it's not true, the younger folks are not clever enough to realize that. Let them believe what they want. Capitalize on it. Make your sage pronouncements and offer your helpful advice as though you *do* know what you're talking about. It's one of the many perks of your age. Cherish it.

There may be a few negatives. You may not see things as sharply as you did a few years back. You may have to say, "What did you say?" a bit more often than when you were younger. You may walk with a slower gait, take longer to get up from a chair, and work a bit harder trying to remember some names, but you can still laugh as hard and as joyously as you ever did. Your sense of humor never wears out.

This book may help you laugh at some of the people who are younger than you, and maybe even a few who are older. Most importantly, though, you will be able to laugh at yourself. That'll keep you young. Remember the words of a beloved comedian who mastered the art of aging, George Burns. He said, "We all have to grow older, but we don't have to grow old."

Have fun.

## Gene Perret & Linda Perret

# REMEMBER,

with age comes wisdom, which is great.

It's all the other stuff that louses it up.

When I was young,
I thought I could
conquer the world.

Now I'd like to go for
best two out of three.

I've lived a long
life. I'm afraid
that when I meet
my maker He
may be younger
than I am.

I'm not

# OLDER

than you are.

I've just been

# YOUNG

longer than you have.

My mother always
taught me to be polite
to my elders.

She never told me
what to do when I

RAN OUT

of them.

I've got aches and pains in parts of my body that I've never even met before.

I've done some bad things, but I've had a good life.

In fact, some of the bad things I've done were probably what made it so good.

I've never tried to be perfect, and i think i've succeeded.

You know you're getting
old when your milk
doesn't come with an
expiration date but
rather a

# LIFETIME GUARANTEE.

No matter how old I get,
I'll always have my

# memories

—even if I have to start
making them up.

The nice thing about being older is that you get to say things that years ago you would have been punished for.

Things get better with age . . . and they are

# 50% OFF

before 6:00 p.m.

Don't laugh at me if
I fall asleep in your
presence. I'm old, and
it's not my fault.

Besides, if you were
more exciting, i might
still be awake.

At my age, I have trouble remembering names, so I try to avoid meeting people who

# have them.

I'm not losing my memory.

I just can't remember names, dates, and a few other things.

Anytime I put
something away in
a safe place, I never
see it again . . . but I
do know it's safe.

I won't tell you my age, but I'll give you a hint:

if i were a tree and you sawed me in half, you'd be counting rings for a month.

I'm exercising more as
I grow older.

That's because my short
walks are starting to feel
like long walks.

Age does have
certain benefits.

Behavior that could
be considered rude,
after a certain age,
becomes quaint.

Age is
nothing more
than the absence
of youth . . . and
a lot of other
things.

Nothing on my body
hurts today.

I think I'll have to
see my

# DOCTOR

about that.

My doctor says I have the body of a thirty-year-old.

That may be true, but it could use a good

# IRONING.

I watched a
commercial on TV.

I don't need the

# medicine

they were advertising, but

I do have all the

# side
# effects

it can cause.

There's only one part of
my body that doesn't hurt
and still works . . . and I
can't remember what
it's used for.

My wife thinks I'm losing my hearing, but that simply isn't true.

I've just gotten really good at ignoring her.

You know you're
getting older when you

CARRY ON
CONVERSATIONS

with whatever
television show
you're watching.

I keep forgetting whether I have a good memory or not.

My doctor says I should exercise more. I said,

"Fine. Do you have a body i can use for that?"

I take so many
**SHORT NAPS,**
I consider them
**LONG BLINKS.**

I'm grumpy when I need a nap, and I'm grumpy when I wake up from a nap.

While I'm napping, I'm **rather pleasant.**

You change as you get older. Some people call it "feisty." I call it "downright ornery."

When I was young, I'd focus all my energy on looking for a hot date.

Now, I get the same thrill from a hot bowl of soup.

I still think I have a

good memory.

That's only because
some of the things I
should have forgotten

i'VE FORGOTTEN
TO FORGET.

Nowadays, getting up
out of a chair tires
me out so much that
I have to

# sit down

for awhile.

You know you're getting
old when you consider
golf a "young man's sport."

When I get out of bed
in the morning, the

# NOISES

my body makes wake
the neighbors.

The memory goes
with age.

When we have the
family over for
dinner now, I ask
them all to wear
**nametags.**

I'm starting to forget
things like where I
put my glasses . . .
and whether I wear
glasses or not.

You know
you're getting old
when you go to
a pharmacy and
buy whatever
they have on sale.

You realize you've gotten older when your grandchildren can have hours of fun connecting the liver spots on your arm.

They say wrinkles
are just

# laugh lines.

Apparently I've lived
a very funny life.

I've reached
the age when
each one of my

# body
# parts

has its own
doctor.

# OLD AGE

is when you seem to
have more wrinkles
than you have skin.

I've lived so long, if I wrote the story of my life, the first volume would be

# dog-eared

by now.

When people ask me what medications I'm on, I tell them, "I take one of everything."

My memory is going.

Last year, I wrote a book of

# MEMOIRS

and it turned out to be a

# PAMPHLET.

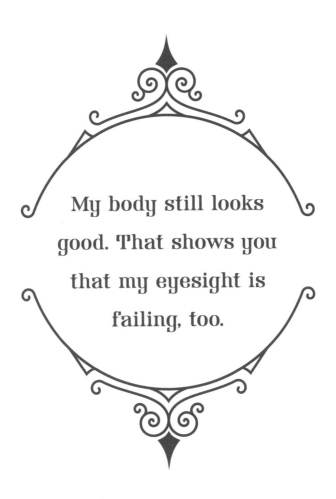

My body still looks good. That shows you that my eyesight is failing, too.

You know how I complain that I can't do a lot of things I could do when I was twenty?

Confession time:

i couldn't do most of them when i was twenty, either.

# You're only young once . . . so drag it out.

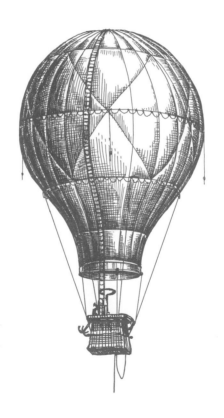

I get all the

# EXERCISE

I need just walking
around the house
trying to remember
where I left my glasses.

I've grown older on purpose.

I wanted to keep seniority over my children.

We don't really get wiser as we get older—we just realize how dumb we were when we were younger.

I used to get up at the crack of dawn.

Now whatever's making that cracking sound is part of my body.

I always exercise
with a friend.

That way I can just
stand there and let
him touch my toes
for me.

My doctor recommended low-impact exercise.

What's more low impact than a

# good,

# brisk

# nap?

I move a little
more slowly now.

That way, if I want to

TURN AROUND

and come home, I won't
have as far to go.

My grandchildren used to think I was all-powerful and all-knowing.

Now they think I'm cute.

My kids have been after
me to do something
different—something I've
never done before.

So I borrowed money
from them.

Someone asked me once, "Who'd want to live to be

one hundred?"

I said, "Probably all of the people who are

ninety-nine."

When I was a youngster,
I got in and out of
trouble all the time.

Now it takes me forever
to get in and out of a car.

You know you're getting old when your grandchildren don't recognize you in the

# family albums

. . . and neither does your spouse.

I walk for a half hour every morning . . .

from the bed to the bathroom and back again.

The only
good thing about
old age is the
senior citizen's
discount.

It's much cheaper to
get into concerts you
don't want to go to.

My wife says i've become
an old grouch.

That sort of implies that i
used to be a young grouch.

My doctor wants me
to walk a mile every day.

I do, but I haven't told
him that I know a

SHORTCUT.

I do lose my temper a lot nowadays . . .

along with my glasses, my car keys, and the shoes I took off last night.

I take a lot of naps.
Many are just light
naps, but I can still
hear the people
laughing at me.

I don't do everything
my doctor tells
me, and I don't
do everything my
preacher tells me.
I do everything my
wife tells me, though.

# I'm old,
# not stupid.

I must look older
than I thought.

My granddaughter asked
me what it was like when
the Earth was

FLAT.

History was more
fun when I was in
school.

We didn't study it;
we lived it.

I'm getting sensitive
about my age.

I'm afraid that when I meet
Saint Peter at the Golden
Gate, I may find out we went
to school together.

Like old wine, I keep getting better with age. But some people claim my cork is starting to dry out.

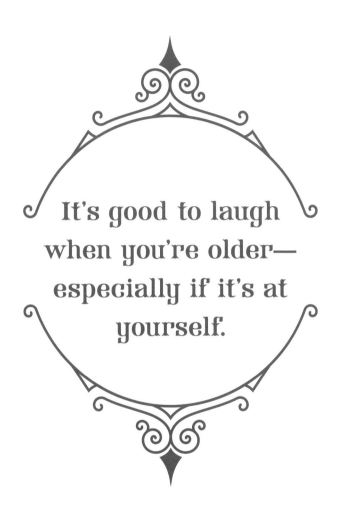

It's good to laugh
when you're older—
especially if it's at
yourself.

I tell my kids I'm not good at babysitting.

They say, "You raised us, didn't you?"

i say, "i rest my case."

My kids say I should take up a hobby. I tell them, "I have a hobby:

**GETTING ON YOUR NERVES."**

With age comes

# wisdom

—the wisdom to
keep your mouth
shut long enough
that people think
you're smart.

They say you're not getting older, you're getting better.

I've got the

# doctor bills

to prove them wrong.

I tried to take up golf as a hobby, but i wasn't very good. So i took up bowling.

i'm still not very good, but i lose the ball less often.

It's nice that husbands
and wives can grow old
together.

That way each one can
blame it on the other.

I'm young at heart. i wish a few other parts of my body would take the hint.

If you're a
bartender
and want a
big tip from
me, ask to
look at my ID.

I don't care if my
memory's failing.
I'm not interested
in remembering
yesterday; I'm
interested in creating
new memories for
tomorrow.

Which I will
quickly forget.

I will admit I've forgotten much of my past. Consider this, though: it may have been upon

legal advice.

I like those stick-on

# NAME TAGS

that they give you at
parties and conventions.

As we've gotten older,
my wife and i have
taken to wearing them
around the house.

I'm at the age when
I can do

# ABSOLUTELY
# NOTHING.

And fortunately, I've
had years of practice
at it.

I've still got one last spurt in me. My wife says,

"Well, let me know when it's coming. i'll wait till afterward to have the carpets cleaned."

My memory is fine.
It's just that many of
the things I've done
aren't that

MEMORABLE.

It seems like my belt line gets higher and higher as I get older. Pretty soon I won't need a belt or suspenders; I can just keep my pants up with my

# teeth.

I can't do a lot of the
things I used to do.

On the other hand, I

# never

should have done some
of those things in the
first place.

If I say something rude
now, people say,

"Aww, he didn't mean
anything by it. He's a
good old coot. He wouldn't
harm a soul."

If I'd said the same
thing when I was young,
they'd say,

"What a jerk!"

One nice thing about being old is that people generally let you have the softest seat in the place.

I don't consider
myself a
"senior citizen."

I consider myself a
"youth survivor."

Some people consider me old because I often forget where I am.

I hesitate to tell them that happened to me a lot in college, too.

i wake up several times
during the night.

i just want to make sure
i'm still here.

After a certain age, pain becomes your new best friend.

You know you're
getting old when
people keep telling you
how young you look.

My

# MIND

never seems to get
older, but my

# BODY

makes up the
difference.

Now that I'm getting older, after I eat, my stomach makes the same noises as my **garbage disposal.**

You know you're
getting old when you
consider

NAPPiNG

a hobby.

I owe my long life to
# good living.

I started last
Thursday.

i attend a

# yoga class

for seniors.

We all assume a certain pose, and after an hour, the instructor comes around and wakes us.

You know you're getting old when the family dog can't believe how much you sleep.

The future is a complete mystery.

But at my age, the present is a little confusing, too.

They say we should live
**one day at a time.**

With frequent naps
and occasional senior
moments, I break it into
even smaller increments.

i may be old, but i like to appear young, so i put racing stripes on my walker.

I can't get old; I've still got

# PLACES TO GO

and

# PEOPLE TO SEE.

Unfortunately, I can't remember how to get there or what the people's names are.

I have a list of three things I want to do with the rest of my life. The first one is to try to remember what the other two are.

My wife likes to visit
**antique stores,**
but I don't.

Why should I? Most of
the things in there are
younger than I am.

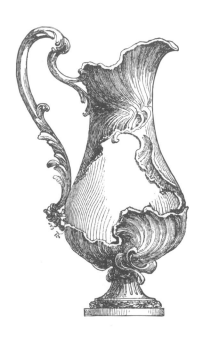

Old age is nature's
way of saying,

"find new ways to
have fun."

When I was young, I could hardly resist **temptation.**

Now that I'm old, I can hardly find it.

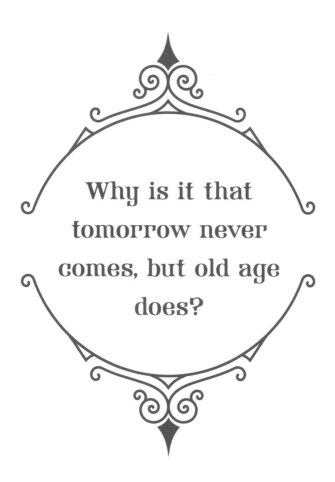

Why is it that tomorrow never comes, but old age does?

You know you're getting older when your children are the same age as some of the things in your

SOCK DRAWER.

You're only young
once. Apparently,
there are no
**free refills.**

# OLD AGE

is a stiff price
to pay for a

# SENIOR
# DISCOUNT.

Old age has a
definite beginning.

It always begins

ten years

from now.

I asked my wife if she'll still love me when I get old.

She said she's been doing that for years now.

My wife and I are
just about the

# SAME AGE

. . . although I wouldn't
dare tell her that.

It just dawned on me . . . i'm older now than i was this same time yesterday.

I walk a little slower than
I used to. That's by design.
It gives me more time to
try to remember where
I'm going and why.

One bad thing about naps is that you can only take one at a time.

I'm happy when I'm sleeping . . . and so is the rest of the family.

I don't seem to be
growing old
GRACEFULLY.

Now I know how the
Roman Colosseum feels.

They say with age comes

# wisdom.

I'm wise enough now to
know that I should have
taken better care of myself
when I was younger.

# Nature compensates.

I noticed that when my hair got thinner, my thinking got fuzzier.

I may be getting on in years, but I can still go out every once in a while and paint the town a light pink.

I hope my ship comes in
soon because my dock
is starting to collapse.

There are

# THREE SIGNS

that prove you're getting older—loss of memory . . . and one other thing.

I don't think i get wiser as i get older, but i will agree that everyone else gets dumber.

You know you're getting old when you forget your grandchildren's names but you can recite all of your MEDICATIONS.

I've reached the age in life when I have more

# doctors

than I have people attending my high school reunions.

You notice different stages
of aging when first athletes
look very young to you . . .
and then policemen . . .
and then presidents . . .
and finally trees.

Old age is never dull.
Anytime you find you
have nothing to do,
you can always take
another pill.

They say there's
no tomorrow.

With my memory
lately, there's no
yesterday, either.

As I get older, I grow more intolerant of annoying people.

Who are the annoying people?
All those who aren't me.

# I

must be getting old.

Over fifty percent of my vocabulary now consists of the names of medications.

As I got older, I became a
TOTAL GROUCH.

Earlier, I guess I was just a
SEMI-GROUCH.

I retired early—about

# ten years

before I left work.

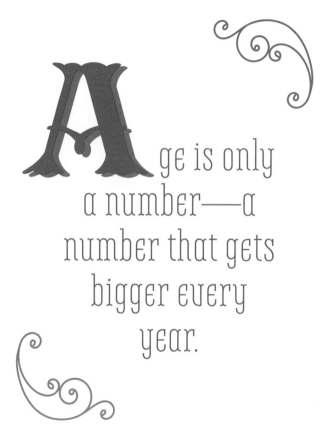

Age is only a number—a number that gets bigger every year.

I get **eight hours** of sleep each night, **eight hours** of sleep each day, and about **eight hours'** worth of naps during my waking hours.

People often ask me,
"What's the best age to be?"

They know I've been
all of them.

# I've reached the age when resting tires me out.

My faculties are failing. Last week, I got lost riding a stationary bike.

I take so many
medications
I've built up an
immunity to

PLACEBOS.

My doctor doesn't give senior discounts, but he does charge me the bulk rate.

I'm not so limber anymore.

The other day, I
pulled a muscle

changing my mind.

I cherish my
# GRAY HAIR.

Many days, it's the
only part of my body
that doesn't hurt.

We don't get wiser as we get older. We just suddenly realize how long we've been dumb.

You know you're getting old when your next doctor's appointment is scheduled for

Monday, Tuesday, and Wednesday.

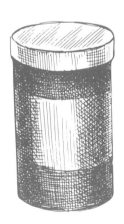

You know you're old
when your

# HIGH SCHOOL REUNION

starts looking like
your doctor's waiting
room.

I move a little slower
now. It takes me

TWICE

as long to go

HALF

as far, and when I get
there, I forget what
I went for.

They say hobbies keep you young.

Right now, my new hobby is trying to remember what my last hobby was.

My hearing is still pretty good. With today's music, I don't exactly consider that a blessing.

If an apple a day keeps the doctor away, then i'm going to need an entire orchard.

You know you're getting old when you take your first few steps after getting out of a chair looking like a

# human question mark.

Just because there's

snow

on the roof doesn't
mean there's not a

fire

in the furnace . . .

Of course, that's
assuming your pilot light
hasn't blown out.

As you get older,
you appreciate the
simple things in life:
your family, financial
security, being able
to get out of a chair
without uttering
"oomph."

You're only as old
as you feel.

I start the day at 32,
but by midafternoon,
I'm pushing 86 . . .
104 if the grandkids
are visiting.

As a kid, I was always
scared of the old man who
lived on our street.

Now I am that old man . . .
and it's even scarier.

I'm not sure why they call them "the golden years." Most of my parts rusted ages ago.

i can do anything today that i could do in my youth; it just takes me a little longer and usually isn't as much fun.

You know you've reached old age when you can tell time by which pills you're taking.

You know you're getting older when fun is anything that doesn't hurt afterwards.

I've become so crabby
in my old age that the
newsboy won't even come
near my house. He calls
me on the phone and
reads the paper to me.

I asked my doctor,

"Can't you give me something to make me feel young again?"

He gave me a pacifier.

I'm still a young man.
At least, I would
be if I were a

# TURTLE.

I seem to get grouchier as I get older. My family says I have a receding personality.

When I was young,
I thought I could
conquer the world.

Nowadays, putting
my socks on by
myself is plenty.

Thank goodness, I'm
still playing with a
# full deck.

I have no idea what
game I'm playing, but
I'm playing it with a
full deck.

They say that age is all in the mind. Then how come that's the only part of my body I don't rub down with

LINIMENT?

I think I've
discovered the
formula for staying
young: limit your
birthdays to less
than one per year.

After a certain age,
temptation is anything that
will keep you up past 9:30.

I can still do anything i could do when i was in my twenties.

Thankfully, though, i always talk myself out of trying it.

You realize you're
old when you admit
that you never
attained the success
you longed for . . .
but several of your
classmates did and
have already retired
from it.

People say that everything gets better with age.

Have you ever taken a good look at a really old

# BANANA?

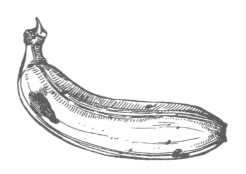

# ABOUT THE AUTHORS

**GENE PERRET** has been a professional comedy writer since the early 1960's. He began his television writing career in 1968 on *The Beautiful Phyllis Diller Show*. Since then he has written or produced many of television's top-rated shows, including *Laugh-In* and *The Carol Burnett Show*. During his career, Gene has collected three Emmys and one Writers Guild Award.

Gene also worked on Bob Hope's writing staff for twenty-eight years, becoming the comic's head-writer and traveling to several war zones for Hope's iconic Christmas shows.

Today, he teaches classes in comedy writing. His hobbies include painting, sketching, and playing the guitar. He paints rather well, sketches adequately, but you don't want to listen to his guitar playing. No one does.

**LINDA PERRET** followed in her father's funny footsteps and sold her first professional joke in 1990.

Since then, she's supplied one-liners and comedy bits for Terry Fator, Bob Hope, Phyllis Diller, Joan Rivers, Yakov Smirnoff, Jimmie Walker, and other stand-up comics.

Linda was a staff writer for the television Emmy Award–winning special celebrating Bob Hope's 90th birthday: "Bob Hope—the First 90 Years."

She has cowritten two collections of business jokes, published by Prentice Hall—*Funny Business* and *Bigshots, Pip-squeaks, and Windbags*. She is the author of HMO's, *Home Remedies and Other Medical Jokes*. Her material has been quoted in *Reader's Digest*, the *National Enquirer*, and *Arizona Highways*.

Linda also launched a joke service called Perrets' Humor Files and continues to operate a newsletter for comedy writers and performers.

# ABOUT FAMILIUS

**Visit Our Website:** www.familius.com

**Join Our Family:** There are lots of ways to connect with us! Subscribe to our newsletters at www.familius.com to receive uplifting daily inspiration, essays from our Pater Familius, a free ebook every month, and the first word on special discounts and Familius news.

**Get Bulk Discounts:** If you feel a few friends and family might benefit from what you've read, let us know and we'll be happy to provide you with quantity discounts. Simply email us at specialorders@familius.com.

www.facebook.com/paterfamilius

@familiustalk, @paterfamilius1

www.pinterest.com/familius

FAMILIUS

The most important work you ever do will be within the walls of your own home.